MW01241531

Be What You Are

Bible Principles for Gender, Roles, and Distinction

N A T H A N   M C C O N N E L L

Bill Rice Ranch Publications
Murfreesboro, TN 37128-4555

ABOUT THE AUTHOR
and this Ministry

Nathan McConnell first became associated with the Bill Rice Ranch as a summer staff counselor. It was during those summer breaks from Bible college that he began to develop a burden for reaching deaf young people. In 2005, Nathan became the Deaf Ministries Director, a position which entails overseeing the deaf camps each summer. Throughout the rest of the year, he teaches regularly, works to promote Deaf Camp in public schools, and assists churches with deaf ministries. Nathan holds a master's degree in Bible Exposition and has authored or edited several other publications from the Bill Rice Ranch. He and his wife Rebekah have two sons, Warren and Walter.

The Ranch was started in 1953 by Evangelist Bill Rice and his wife Cathy as a way to reach the Deaf with the message of salvation. The Ranch now holds week-long sessions all summer in three separate programs—Deaf, Junior, and Teen. These programs run simultaneously, allowing churches to bring young people from all three groups while only making one trip. The Ranch also conducts family camps and special seasonal events each year.

FOR MORE INFORMATION
about the Bill Rice Ranch,
please call 615-893-2767,
write to the Bill Rice Ranch,
627 Bill Rice Ranch Rd., Murfreesboro, TN 37128,
or visit the website at www.billriceranch.org.

Contents

INTRODUCTION
Cultural Chaos!. 7

CHAPTER ONE
Embracing Your Identity, Part 1 11

CHAPTER TWO
Embracing Your Identity, Part 2 17

CHAPTER THREE
Playing Your Role, Part 1 29

CHAPTER FOUR
Playing Your Role, Part 2 37

CHAPTER FIVE
Displaying Your Gender, Part 1 45

CHAPTER SIX
Displaying Your Gender, Part 2 51

CONCLUSION
At the Heart of the Issue 59

Notes 63

Cultural Chaos!

"Have ye not read, that he which made them at the beginning made them male and female...?"
—Matthew 19:4

Kathy and her husband David welcomed their third child into the world on January 1, 2011. They named the baby Storm. The baby was born with beautiful blue eyes, fair hair, and chubby cheeks. There is absolutely no question that the baby is healthy and beautiful. The only real question on everyone's minds is: *what is it?* You see, the parents have decided to keep the baby's gender a secret and to let him/her decide for himself/herself when he/she is ready! Though obviously the parents, two siblings, and two midwives who helped with the at-home delivery know the actual gender of the baby, Kathy and David feel that it is important not to stigmatize the child with preconceived cultural ideas about gender by telling it what it is.[1]

This actual reported news story serves to highlight the fact that our society debates the importance of gender. Confusion over what constitutes manhood and womanhood, or how to define male and female abound. *What makes a man a man? What makes a woman a woman? Why can't one just choose to be the other?* In fact, the ongoing debate over same-sex marriage is merely a symptom of the underlying issue of gender confusion. *What does it really matter? They ask. Aren't we just programmed to believe and feel a certain way because of cultural pressures?* More and more in our society, gender is being defined not by what you are, but by what you feel that you are. The Planned Parenthood website, for example, devotes a page to "Gender Identity" with this explanation:

> *"Whether we are women or men is not determined by our* [physical bodies]. *Our gender includes a complex mix of beliefs, behaviors, and characteristics... Are you feminine, masculine, both, or neither?"*[2]

I quote Planned Parenthood not to identify them as the problem. They are merely addressing, and supporting, a problem that has infiltrated western society, namely the confusion over what we are.

As crazy as the notion sounds, deciding your gender based on feeling is being propagated by schools, universities, special interest groups, music, television, and even some religious organizations (though they lie outside the boundaries of traditional Christianity). These groups seek to make the gender question open to interpretation. Male/female uniqueness and distinctions are downplayed or even discouraged ("girls are as good as boys," etc.). Traditional roles are ridiculed (stay-at-home moms, etc.). Often on television programs, those whose lifestyles contradict Christian moral values are portrayed as heroic, normal, or "just as good as everyone else."

As Christians, we can see that behind all of this confusion lies our culture's denial of God's authority. Fundamentally, what people understand about themselves (e.g., gender) is a reflection of what they believe, or don't believe, about God. If there is no Creator, then *what am I?* and *why am I here?* are questions open to debate. If there is no Designer, I get to decide how my body is used. If there is no Divine Authority, I get the final say on what's right for me. *I* take the place of God when *I* choose not to believe in Him. And when a person becomes the final authority for himself, nothing can be forbidden him.

But the world should see the answers to all of its questions through the living example of the church. The church is, after all, "the pillar and ground of the truth" (I Timothy 3:15). As people who, contrary to the surrounding culture, accept God's authority, the church should be the most settled on *what they are* and *what that means*. On the question of gender, however, even good Christians need help. In this society, churches have not always clearly or helpfully addressed issues related to gender (dress, appropriate activities, etc.), and the gender-specific roles that follow a biblical pattern. Plus, the visible display of distinction between the genders has been a hot-button issue for decades. On the questions of *being male or female* and *acting masculine or feminine*, surely the church should have its act together, right?

In order for the church to rightly display gender, roles, and distinction to the world, we must look to the Scriptures and rediscover what God has said regarding them. Ephesians 5:15 challenges Christians to "walk circumspectly, not as fools, but as wise." Living circumspectly as a wise person means behaving accurately in the light of God's revealed will (verses 16-17 bear this out). Therefore, knowing God's mind on identity, roles, and distinction will lead us to more accurately display what God has made us to be both in the church and to the world.

In the following chapters, we will look to the Bible and answer the question of identity, in order to embrace what God made us to be. We will explore roles so that we can live out what God made us to be. And finally, we will tackle the subject of distinction and displaying what God made us to be. These answers from God's Word can help us to both show and tell to the world God's design for His Creation.

CHAPTER ONE

Embracing Your Identity, Part I

*"And God said, Let us make man in our image, after our like-
ness... So God created man in his own image, in the image of
God created he him; male and female created he them."*
—Genesis 1:26-27

A 2012 Gallup survey of 121,190 people reported that 3.4% of
the American adult population identifies themselves as lesbian,
gay, bisexual, or transgender (LGBT). The study also found
that 8.3% of women and 4.6% of men between the ages of 18-29
identified themselves as LGBT. This age group represented the
highest percentage of any age group in the survey.[3] Though
news media and television programs would have us believe
the homosexual population is much higher, this statistic is still

staggering because it brings to light the epidemic of confusion surrounding gender identity. Gender identity to the LGBT community is subjective (figuring it out based on feeling), not objective (knowing it based on fact).

WHAT YOU ARE

Your identity is, essentially, who and what you are. Recognizing your identity as male or female is entry-level identification. Though your perception of everything that identity means will grow over time, you have to have a foundation if you are to mature. Unlike the world which searches for an understanding of its identity through exploration and experimentation, a Christian has Divine Revelation to give him understanding. So, for a Christian whose authority is the Bible, there is a very short answer to the question of gender identity: *You are what God made you.*

"...*male and female created he them.*"—Genesis 1:27

"...*male and female created he them.*"—Genesis 5:2

"...*he which made them at the beginning made them male and female....*"—Matthew 19:4

"...*from the beginning of the creation God made them male and female.*"—Mark 10:6

A person's identity as male or female is the Creator's decision, not an inventive determination. You are either male or female, and what you were created is what you are. To question what you are by creation, or to reject what you are by creation, is to question and refuse the God Who made you.

I can hear someone objecting now: *So what you're saying is that I'm just the sum of all my physical parts?* No, there is much more to you than just your anatomy. I am saying two things. First, if you are going to gain any understanding at all about your identity, you do have to start there. God *only* created male and female, and we are born as one or the other. And—guess what—the doctors and nurses already made a call about *what you are* when you were born. Though we grow to discover *what it means* to be male and female, we cannot dispute that *we are* male or female. Second, accepting the fact of our identity by creation, we need to embrace that identity. It is what we are, and running from that fact can only lead to confusion and immorality, as we will see.

So what does embracing your identity as male or female mean?

GOD'S PERSPECTIVE: EQUALITY

First, embracing your identity does not mean accepting either an inferior or superior position. Often Christians have swallowed the line that "girls can play sports as good as boys," thereby making boys the standard for girls. *Where is that in the Bible?!* Since when should girls aspire to compete with boys? That kind of thinking is absolutely contrary to the Scriptures. What we learn about God's initial creation of mankind is that male and female are created equal in three aspects:

1. **Male and female equally bear God's image.** Being made in the image of God was not the special privilege of Adam. The Bible says that "man" (read *mankind*) was made in the image of God, bearing His likeness. Both male and female exhibit intellect, the capacity to reason and communicate, and the ability to relate to someone other than themselves.

2. **Male and female are equal in relation to God.** God does not view male and female differently with regard to personal responsibility, or in relationship to Him. Both have been given responsibilities that God expects each to fulfill. Both have the privilege to know God personally and to obey Him. Embracing what we are does not limit our capacity to know God in any way. Both male and female can know Him just the same.

3. **Male and female are equal in relation to one another.** Woman was "taken out of Man" (Genesis 2:23) in order to be a suitable helper for Adam. But she was not made to be a servant to Adam. Together, they were each in

their respective roles to contribute to fulfilling God's command to "be fruitful," to "subdue" the earth, and to "have dominion over… every living thing" (Genesis 1:28). The male's role as *leader* (we will discuss roles later) doesn't make him better. The female's role as *helper* does not make her worse. Embracing your identity as male or female, then, does not make you less or more than someone else.

Since the fall of man, male and female share in the equal privilege of salvation. The New Testament makes it clear that both men and women are equal in the opportunity to be saved and in the experience of everything that salvation means.

> *"There is neither Jew nor Greek, there is neither bond nor free, there is neither male nor female: for ye are all one in Christ Jesus."*—Galatians 3:28

Therefore, embracing your identity does not mean accepting a position that is inferior or superior to anyone else. God's perspective is that male and female are equal in their worth and standing before Him, and in relation to one another as human beings created in God's image.

Embracing Your Identity, Part 2

"Nevertheless, to avoid fornication, let every man have his own wife, and let every woman have her own husband."
—I Corinthians 7:2

After World War II, American culture succeeded in promoting the idea that masculinity (the male role) is promiscuity, and that femininity (the female role) is chastity. Then, in the 1960s, the "sexual revolution" supposedly set everyone free to be promiscuous. After all, the girls could be "just as good as" the boys, right? Enter feminism, the homosexual movement, and gender confusion! But a Christian, who understands his identity based on Authority, must recognize the moral boundaries established by that Authority as well.

GOD'S PURPOSE: MORALITY

Embracing your identity will mean submitting to the moral boundaries of what you are. If you will trust God's Word for what you are, trust His guidelines for protecting what you are. *What are God's moral boundaries?*

First, all homosexual activity is forbidden. Despite the world's twisted attack on people who believe homosexuality is sin, God's design at Creation and His plainly stated commands affirm this prohibition. God made them male and female with the expressed intent that they were meant for each other in physical union, that is, the male for the female and the female for the male. This is clearly God's creative intent:

> *"God said unto them, Be fruitful, and multiply, and replenish the earth...."*—Genesis 1:28

> *"...they* [a man and his wife] *shall be one flesh. And they were both naked, the man and his wife, and were not ashamed."* —Genesis 2:24-25

Homosexuality does away with God's design for male and female by intending male for male and female for female. This is a denial of God's creative design. Homosexual acts cannot and do not fulfill God's command for mankind to "be fruitful, and multiply." Furthermore, as we will see in the discussion of roles, the male and the female each bring their own dynamic to the family. A family unit composed of two dads or two moms cannot mimic a scriptural family dynamic. Therefore, homosexuality is contrary to God's design for His creation.

Beyond the plain design that God had for male and female at Creation are God's repeated prohibitions against homosexual behavior throughout the entire Bible: Old *and* New Testaments. Some have argued that the prohibition against homosexuality was an Old Testament law that was abolished in the New Testament era of grace. As we shall see, those who argue that case have not made a thorough search of their Bibles. Here is what the Christian's Authority has to say about homosexuality:

> *"And the LORD said… their* [Sodom and Gomorrah's] *sin is very grievous;"*—Genesis 18:20

> *"…the men of Sodom, compassed the house round, both old and young… And they called unto Lot, and said unto him, Where are the men which came in to thee this night? Bring them out unto us, that we may know them."*—Genesis 19:4-5

From these verses we see that the grievous sin of Sodom and Gomorrah was the men's homosexual behavior.

> *"Thou shalt not lie with mankind, as with womankind: it is abomination."*—Leviticus 18:22

> *"If a man also lie with mankind, as he lieth with a woman, both of them have committed an abomination...."*
> —Leviticus 20:13

The word *abomination* is a strong word. Anything that compromises God's perfect sacrifice, God's moral absolutes, or God's unique position is an abomination. Therefore, homosexual behavior violates the moral absolutes found in God's Creation and Law.

> *"...the men of the city, certain sons of Belial* [the devil], *beset the house round about... saying, Bring forth the man that came into thine house, that we may know him."*
> —Judges 19:22

Those who were obviously associated with the devil (Belial) are here engaging in homosexual behavior. Don't take that to mean that all homosexuals are Satanists. It does mean that those who engage in homosexual behavior are in direct violation of God's creative design and live in outright rebellion to God's unique position as Authority and Creator, as Satan does.

> *"And there were also sodomites in the land: and they did according to all the abominations of the nations which the LORD cast out before the children of Israel."*—I Kings 14:24

"And he [Asa] took away the sodomites out of the land, and removed all the idols that his fathers had made."
—I Kings 15:12

"And he [Josiah] brake down the houses of the sodomites, that were by the house of the LORD, where the women wove hangings for the grove."—II Kings 23:7

The presence of homosexuals in the land was a sign of significant religious and moral decline for the nation of Israel. King Asa and King Josiah, we are told, cleansed the land specifically of practicing religious homosexuals (those who prostituted themselves in the service of a false idol).

"For the wrath of God is revealed from heaven against all ungodliness and unrighteousness of men... when they knew God, they glorified him not as God, neither were thankful... God also gave them up to uncleanness through the lusts of their own hearts, to dishonour their own bodies between themselves: who changed the truth of God into a lie, and worshipped and served the creature more than the Creator... For this cause God gave them up unto vile affections: for even their women did change the natural use into that which is against nature: and likewise also the men, leaving the natural use of the woman, burned in their lust one toward another; men with men working that which is unseemly...."—Romans 1:18, 21, 24-27

This New Testament passage graphically describes the affections and actions of homosexuals. What begins as the Creation's refusal to respect God as Creator ends in the "vile affections," the "lusts," and the "unseemly" activity of homosexuality. Notice that the slippery slope begins with their not honoring Him as God and their not being thankful (v. 21). We honor and appreciate God as Creator when we accept what He created us to be. Failing to embrace what we are puts us on the path to immorality. Failing to submit to His moral boundaries makes us immoral.

> *"Know ye not that the unrighteous shall not inherit the kingdom of God? Be not deceived: neither fornicators, nor idolaters, nor adulterers, nor effeminate, nor abusers of themselves with mankind, nor thieves, nor covetous, nor drunkards, nor revilers, nor extortioners, shall inherit the kingdom of God."*—I Corinthians 6:9-10

Though space would not allow us to explain the broader point Paul is making in this passage, it is enough for the scope of this current study to point out that "effeminate" and "abusers of themselves with mankind" are direct references to homosexuals. These are "unrighteous."

> *"But we know that the law is good, if a man use it lawfully; knowing this, that the law is not made for a righteous man, but for the lawless and disobedient, for the ungodly and for sinners, for unholy and profane, for murderers of fathers and*

murderers of mothers, for manslayers, for whoremongers, for them that defile themselves with mankind, for menstealers, for liars, for perjured persons, and if there be any other thing that is contrary to sound doctrine."—I Timothy 1:8-10

Again, the entire scope of these verses is broader than our space. But we see Paul referring to "them that defile themselves with mankind" (the same Greek word used in I Corinthians 6:9) as being in a different category than the "righteous." Homosexuals engage in activity that does not conform to the moral laws of God.

"*Even as Sodom and Gomorrha, and the cities about them in like manner, giving themselves over to fornication, and going after strange flesh, are set forth for an example, suffering the vengeance of eternal fire.*"—Jude 7

Here Sodom and Gomorrah are referenced as being punished for "giving themselves over to fornication" (one Greek word that means *utterly unchaste*) and "going after strange flesh," that is turning away from God's design (male for female) to bodies forbidden to them (male with male). For this they suffered "the vengeance of eternal fire"—the fiery vengeance of an eternal God.

Having embraced your identity as male or female, strengthen that identity by submitting to God's moral boundaries. That means seeing homosexual acts for what they are: forbidden by God.

Second, all sexual acts outside of marriage are forbidden. God's creative intent *generally* was male for female and female for male. They were made for each other. But, more *specifically*, His intent of the male/female relationship was husband for wife and wife for husband. Adam and Eve were not only the first man and woman; they were the first husband and wife!

> *"Therefore shall a man leave his father and his mother, and shall cleave unto his wife: and they shall be one flesh."*
> —Genesis 2:24

Adam didn't even have a father and mother, but future boys and girls would. In the Garden, God instituted marriage as the approved condition for male/female relations. God did not command *men* and *women* to "be fruitful, and multiply, and replenish the earth." He commanded a husband and a wife to do so. Paul reiterates this:

> *"Now concerning the things whereof ye wrote unto me: It is good for a man not to touch a woman. Nevertheless, to avoid fornication, let every man have his own wife, and let every woman have her own husband."*—I Corinthians 7:1-2

The act of marriage is reserved for marriage. Outside of marriage, a physical relationship between a man and a woman is called "fornication," and it is forbidden by God in numerous passages throughout the Scriptures (Exodus 20:14; Leviticus 18:20; Deuteronomy 5:18; 22:22-24; Ephesians 5:3-5; Colossians

3:5; I Thessalonians 4:3-4). God promises strong punishment for those who ignore this moral boundary that He has established.

> *"Marriage is honourable in all, and the bed* [marriage act] *undefiled: but whoremongers and adulterers God will judge."*— Hebrews 13:4

The consequences of sexual immorality are dire. Consider the commands of the Scripture to put to death anyone who willingly engages in adulterous activity.

> *"If a man be found lying with a woman married to an husband, then they shall both of them die, both the man that lay with the woman, and the woman: so shalt thou put away evil from Israel."*—Deuteronomy 22:22

Some might say, "That's a cruel and outdated law! What a despicable and hateful rule!" We certainly do not live under the fear of such consequences today (culturally or otherwise). But let's remember that many Old Testament laws were the shadow of a greater reality. Sure, the Law was given to outline God's principles for how a holy people will behave. A holy people will hate sin and drive it from them at any cost. But the penalty of physical death for sexual immorality represented a death that went far deeper.

> *"But whoso committeth adultery with a woman lacketh understanding: he that doeth it destroyeth his own soul. A*

wound and dishonour shall he get; and his reproach shall not be wiped away."—Proverbs 6:32-33

"*Flee fornication. Every sin that a man doeth is without the body; but he that committeth fornication sinneth against his own body.*"—I Corinthians 6:18

Sexual immorality damages your conscience, scars your mind, affects your reputation, and inflicts harm on your body (Deuteronomy 22:22; Proverbs 6:32-33; I Corinthians 6:18). Do those who engage in such activity know God's judgment? You'd better believe it.

Submitting to God's moral boundaries strengthens your identity as either male or female and protects you, allowing you to mature in that identity.

GOD'S PASSION: HIS GLORY

Third, embracing your identity means trusting God as your Creator and Guide for this life. Having seen from the Scriptures what God says about gender identity and boundaries, no matter how you feel or what someone may have suggested to you, know that you can trust your loving Creator. He is good. He knows best. He made you *what you are* for a reason. And, at the end of the day, His reason is for *His glory*.

The word *glory* in the Bible has three meanings. First, it can mean a bright light—when the angels appeared the night Jesus was born, for instance. "The glory of the Lord shone round about them" (Luke 2:9). Second, it can mean praise. "Glory to God in the highest" (Luke 2:14). Finally, it can mean a unique position. "All have sinned and come short of the glory of God" (Romans 3:23). When our behavior sheds light on God's unique position so that He is praised, God is being glorified.

Though there are other reasons God made you male or female, His ultimate purpose was that you would live as He made you, trusting Him entirely with His choice, so that His unique position as Creator could be seen and praised. He will get that glory by working in you and through you.

> *"And as Jesus passed by, he saw a man which was blind from his birth. And his disciples asked him, saying, Master, who did sin, this man, or his parents, that he was born blind? Jesus answered, Neither hath this man sinned, nor his parents: but that the works of God should be made manifest in him."*—John 9:1-3

This man was born blind. That was his condition at birth. The reason for his being born blind did not have anything to do with him or his parents. His blindness was part of God's design to manifest His work. Now, hopefully you don't see your gender as a handicap! The principle is that *you are what you are so that God can show His works through you.*

And God not only has His reason, but remember that He is good. His intentions for you and toward you are good and hopeful.

> *"For I know the thoughts that I think toward you, saith the LORD, thoughts of peace, and not of evil, to give you an expected end."*—Jeremiah 29:11

God's passion for the Christian is that we glorify Him. We cannot do that by denying what He made us or by ignoring His moral boundaries. So, what are you? Embrace that identity, strengthen it by submitting to God's moral boundaries, and then glorify God through your identity by accurately playing your role, a subject we will look into next.

CHAPTER THREE

Playing Your Role, Part I

"And God blessed them, and God said unto them, Be fruitful, and multiply, and replenish the earth, and subdue it: and have dominion over the fish of the sea, and over the fowl of the air, and over every living thing that moveth upon the earth."
—Genesis 1:28

"Unto the woman he said, I will greatly multiply thy sorrow and thy conception; in sorrow thou shalt bring forth children; and thy desire shall be to thy husband, and he shall rule over thee. And unto Adam he said, Because thou hast hearkened unto the voice of thy wife, and hast eaten of the tree... cursed is the ground for thy sake; in sorrow shalt thou eat of it all the days of thy life... In the sweat of thy face shalt thou eat bread, till thou return unto the ground...."
—Genesis 3:16-19

I knew who the actor was, and I knew that his character on the weekly primetime sitcom was a sleazy, with-a-different-woman-every-week womanizer. Though I had never seen the television program (nor do I intend to), what little I had caught from commercials during Sunday afternoon football had brought me to these obvious conclusions. Then a bombshell was dropped on me: *the actor is actually a homosexual!* The role he is playing for the sitcom does not reflect the person he is. (Incidentally, his homosexuality does not reflect the person God made him either.)

God intends for *what you are* to be clearly connected to *what you do*. What you are is your identity; what you do is your role. Though male and female are equal in bearing God's image and in relation to God, they are not the same in function, responsibility, or role. That means that though male and female are equal in relation to one another as being human and bearing God's image, God does not expect or desire them to do the same things in behavior toward one another and in fulfilling His creation mandate ("be fruitful," "multiply," etc.) The male has a role to play. The female has a role to play. These roles are different yet equally important in God's Creation.

THE FACT OF DISTINCT ROLES

That male and female are to play different roles in God's Creation was evident from the beginning. The creation mandate and the fact that there were two parties involved in fulfilling it (male and female), point to the fact that each had a part to play. For example, the command "be fruitful, and multiply," coupled with the fact that standing there were a male and a female, requires that each play a different, distinct role in order to fulfill that command. One would "father" a child; one would bear the child.

Some claim that male headship is a result of the curse of sin. But the curse is actually further proof as to the distinct roles God intended for male and female from the beginning. Sin did not destroy God's intent for Creation, but it did mar that intent. The joy of childbirth (something assigned to the woman by the sheer nature of her anatomy!) would be marred by pain and sorrow. The joy of her assisting relationship to the man would be marred by the strife of desiring to subdue him. The joy of work associated with providing for the family would be marred by sweat and difficulty. Each of these curses corresponds to the original creation mandate to "be fruitful, and multiply" and to "subdue" the earth and "have dominion" (Genesis 1:28). *God's curse for each reflected the marring that sin had brought to their distinctive roles.*

What are the roles that God intended, and intends, for male and female?

THE FUNCTION OF DISTINCT ROLES: MALE

The masculine role, as God intended it, can be summed up in two words: *leader* and *provider*.

Male as the Leader

God's intention for male headship (role as leader) is confirmed by several important facts.

First, the entire human race was named *man*. "And God said, Let us make *man* in our image" (Genesis 1:26, emphasis added). This statement is also repeated in Genesis 5:1. Then, Genesis 5:2 takes the case even further by stating:

> *"Male and female created he them; and blessed them, and* called their name Adam, *in the day when they were created."*—Genesis 5:2 [emphasis added]

By identifying the entire human race with the title "man," and by recognizing the male/female relationship with Adam's name, God showed that He intended the male to be the head, especially in relation with the woman.

Second, the man *named* the woman.

> *"And Adam said, This is now bone of my bones, and flesh of my flesh: she shall be called Woman, because she was taken out of Man."*—Genesis 2:23

Adam had previously exercised his role as head of God's creation by naming all the animals. This he did at God's behest that he find "a help meet for him." Eve who, unlike the animals, *was* a suitable helper for Adam. As she stands before him, he exercises *that* naming authority with her. Surely this is an expression of Adam's sense of his role as leader. Not only that, but Adam's first act of obedience after the curse (a result of his forfeiting his headship) was to reclaim his role as leader by renaming his wife Eve in light of God's new promise of a coming "seed" (Genesis 3:20).

Third, Adam bears the blame for the whole calamity of sin.

> *"Wherefore, as by one man sin entered into the world, and death by sin; and so death passed upon all men, for that all have sinned."*—Romans 5:12

When God returned to the garden, He called for Adam (Genesis 3:9). And though the woman receives a curse because of sin, a reason for Adam's curse is plainly stated: "because thou hast hearkened unto the voice of thy wife" (Genesis 3:17). Adam surrendered his rightful role as leader to his wife, allowing disobedience to God's command. He bore the responsibility of sin because he had the responsibility to lead.

Fourth, the New Testament reaffirms the intent of Creation, that the man should lead.

"But I would have you know, that the head of every man is Christ; and the head of the woman is the man; and the head of Christ is God."—I Corinthians 11:3

"But I suffer not a woman to teach, nor to usurp authority over the man, but to be in silence. For Adam was first formed, then Eve."—I Timothy 2:12-13

These passages deal with authority in the church, not marriage. What is especially clear from the I Corinthians passage is that the leadership role does not equal superiority, but authority. God the Father occupies a "higher" authority than the Son, just as the man occupies a place of authority "higher" than the woman. The issue is not superiority versus inferiority; it is simply a matter of position in an authority structure. In I Timothy, Paul sees the role of a teacher as a position of authority. Therefore it would be contradictory to God's original intent (since "Adam was first formed") for the woman to occupy that position over a man. Creative order signifies creative intent.

As leader, a man should take the initiative in decision making, planning, discipline of children, ministry, intimacy with his wife, etc. In short, he should *take charge*. Too many men are guilty of passivity and fail to fulfill this aspect of their God-given role.

Male as the Provider

Working in order to provide was built into the male role from the beginning.

> *"And the LORD God took the man, and put him into the garden of Eden to dress it and to keep it."*—Genesis 2:15

When God placed Adam into the garden, He told him that he could freely partake of all the trees of the garden except for one. The work of tending the garden was rewarded with the enjoyment of partaking of the garden. In his partaking of the garden, Adam would have, no doubt, shared with his wife and children. God's curse on Adam reaffirms that he was considered the primary breadwinner. Work was not a result of the curse, difficulty was.

Together, Genesis 2:15 and Genesis 3:18, where God tells Adam he would now eat bread by the sweat of his brow, make clear that the Genesis 1:28 command to "subdue" the earth was specifically meant for the male role. This is not to say that a woman working outside the home is unbiblical (we will address that issue when we consider the female role), nor does it question a woman's *ability* to work. But it cannot be disputed that the role most responsible for the work and provision for the family was intended to be the man.

As provider, a man should work for the financial well-being and sustenance of his family and should consider how else he can contribute to their needs (protection of wife and children, wife's need for intimacy, etc.).

This leader/provider role is God's original intent for the male gender, especially in relation to a female. Any mistreatment of women or children (verbal, physical, or sexual) is a direct violation of God's intent for the male role. Age and marital status will dictate its practical expression, but any man seeking to fulfill his God-given responsibilities must take his role seriously.

CHAPTER FOUR

Playing Your Role, Part 2

"Unto the woman he said, I will greatly multiply thy sorrow and thy conception; in sorrow thou shalt bring forth children; and thy desire shall be to thy husband, and he shall rule over thee."
—Genesis 3:16

"Wives, submit yourselves unto your own husbands, as unto the Lord. For the husband is the head of the wife…."
—Ephesians 5:22-23

Former Harvard University president Lawrence H. Summers created a firestorm of controversy in January 2005 when he speculated out loud to a mixed group of scientists that the reason more women don't occupy positions in math and science departments could "stem from biological distinctions between the sexes." Another of his considerations was that most women play the role of wife and mother, thereby limiting the amount of time they can dedicate to their work.[4] Summers resigned as Harvard's president on February 21, 2006.

University professors, like the ones who pounced on Summers's comments, would like to convince us that differences in male and female roles can be traced to *cultural tradition*. As we will see, the female role of wife and mother is a biblical pattern, not a societal trap.

THE FUNCTION OF DISTINCT ROLES: FEMALE

Just as the male role can be described with the words *leader* and *provider*, the female role can be described with the words *helper* and *caregiver*.

Female as the Helper

The whole creation of the woman surrounds the search of a suitable helper ("a help meet") for Adam.

> "… *but for Adam there was not found an help meet for him…. And the rib, which the LORD God had taken from man, made he a woman, and brought her unto the man. And Adam said, This is now bone of my bones, and flesh of my*

flesh: she shall be called Woman, because she was taken out of Man."—Genesis 2:20, 22-23

Adam could not fulfill God's intended purpose for mankind by himself. No member of the animal kingdom was compatible. Another male would not have sufficed. It was the woman who fulfilled this role of a helper "meet" (fitting, suitable) for Adam. The New Testament reaffirms this connection for the female role:

"For the man is not of the woman; but the woman of the man. Neither was the man created for the woman; but the woman for the man."—I Corinthians 11:8-9

The female role is that of helper, especially in relation to a male. According to the Bible, a female fulfills her God-given responsibility by submitting to the headship of the male, and by assisting him in carrying out God's creation mandate. In this way she is a *helper.*

This is a great paradox: male/female equality and male headship/female submission. Man and woman are equal as human beings, but they are not equal in their role. Feminists wrongly assume that the submissive role equals inferiority. But a woman is no more inferior in her role as helper than God is when He fulfills the role of Helper in our lives, or Jesus, Who "came not to be ministered unto, but to minister," was in His.

As helper, a woman should assist the man in his God-given role as leader by respectfully offering opinions, suggestions, and recommendations in the decision making process, by supporting his final decision, and by doing what she can at home (or work) to support his position in the workplace or in the community.

Female as the Caregiver

As we mentioned earlier, the curses of Genesis 3 make sense in the context of God's original intent for each gender.

> *"Unto the woman he said, I will greatly multiply thy sorrow and thy conception; in sorrow thou shalt bring forth children; and thy desire shall be to thy husband, and he shall rule over thee."Genesis 3:16*

In God's directive to the woman, He makes plain that her responsibility is that of a wife and mother. Her suitability for the male corresponds to her being a wife (Genesis 2:20-25). Her childbearing correlates to her being a mother. Though the male is ultimately responsible for the teaching and training of the children (Ephesians 6:4), the female engages in instructing and guiding them also, while keeping the house.

> *"I will therefore that the younger women marry, bear children, guide the house, give none occasion to the adversary to speak reproachfully."*—I Timothy 5:14

"...teach the young women to be sober, to love their husbands, to love their children, to be discreet, chaste, keepers at home, good, obedient to their own husbands, that the word of God be not blasphemed."—Titus 2:4-5

God's intended arena for the woman is the home because that is where the children are.[5] So, what about Proverbs 31? Isn't the virtuous woman a working woman? Yes, the caregiver aspect of the female role does not prohibit her working outside the home. In fact, the Proverbs 31 passage has the woman's responsibility to her family fully in view.

"She will do him [her husband] *good and not evil all the days of her life."*—Proverbs 31:12

"She is not afraid of the snow for her household: for all her household are clothed with scarlet."—Proverbs 31:21

"She looketh well to the ways of her household, and eateth not the bread of idleness. Her children arise up, and call her blessed; her husband also, and he praiseth her."
—Proverbs 31:27-28

The Proverbs 31 woman has a virtuous character, in part, because she faithfully fulfills her role as caregiver to her family.

Ruth is an example of a widow, or single lady, working outside the home for the benefit of her "family," in this case Naomi (Ruth 2:2-3). Ruth 2:8 indicates that Boaz had other "maidens" (single ladies) gleaning in his field as well. The central question is: *How does working outside the home contribute to a woman's fulfilling her role as caregiver to her family?*

As caregiver, a woman should tend the children by providing protection, instruction, and guidance in the husband's absence and should seek to wholly satisfy her husband (emotionally, socially, and physically).

Some may argue that the helper/caregiver role of the female applies only to a wife because "the woman" God created was a wife to Adam. We must understand that the creative intent for woman as helper/caregiver applies to the female gender. Even Lawrence Summers (mentioned earlier) relayed the story of his daughter who, when given two trucks for her playtime, imagined one as "Daddy" truck and the other as "Baby" truck![6] The giving of care is a natural expression of the female gender.

I Corinthians 14 testifies, as well, that the headship of man and the submission of woman transcend the marriage relationship. They are innate to the female gender.

> "Let your women keep silence in the churches: for it is not permitted unto them to speak; but they are commanded to be under obedience, as also saith the law. And if they will learn any thing, let them ask their husbands at home: for it is a shame for women to speak in the church."
> —I Corinthians 14:34-35

This is not a blanket command for women to stop talking in church gatherings. It is not a prohibition against women giving a testimony in mixed company. Something was going on during the assembling of the Corinthian church that undermined male headship and female submission. As with many other activities in the Corinthian worship service, Paul was correcting them on it.

Whereas a man's mistreatment of women and children contradicts his role as leader/provider, a woman's disrespect toward a man and the neglect of children contradict her role as helper/caregiver. Though, as with the male, age and marital status will dictate how it is practically carried out, the female role is a helper/caregiver.

CHAPTER FIVE

Displaying Your Gender, Part 1

"Neither shalt thou go up by steps unto mine altar, that thy
nakedness be not discovered thereon."
—Exodus 20:26

"In like manner also, that women adorn themselves in modest
apparel, with shamefacedness and sobriety; not with broided
hair, or gold, or pearls, or costly array; But (which becometh
women professing godliness) with good works."
—I Timothy 2:9-10

The American film industry has regularly tried to normalize
gender confusion. Their humor frequently makes light of the
inability to determine a person's gender based on appearance.

An old Saturday Night Live skit about Pat, an individual with an indeterminate gender, is just one example. The scripting of the Pat segments plays up the awkwardness that *actually occurs* when someone's gender is not clearly discernible.

Biblically, *what we are* and *what we do* is further supported by *how we appear*. Old Testament regulations regarding the attire of the high priest and of the priests are examples of clearly displaying role with attire. A negative example is the harlot, who was clearly identified by her clothing. When *how we appear* contradicts *what we are*, confusion rules. Jacob's deception of Isaac by pretending to be Esau and the Pharisees' pretense of spirituality by their dress and behavior are just two examples. Consider also the example of a worldly Christian:

> *"I pray not that thou shouldest take them out of the world, but that thou shouldest keep them from the evil. They are not of the world, even as I am not of the world."*—John 17:15-16

> *"Love not the world, neither the things that are in the world. If any man love the world, the love of the Father is not in him."*—I John 2:15

> *"But he that lacketh these things* [spiritual growth] *is blind, and cannot see afar off, and hath forgotten that he was purged from his old sins."*—II Peter 1:9

Before God, a Christian is robed in the righteousness of Jesus Christ. He is different by his position before God, and should display that difference to the world by his actions (James 2:14-26). Someone who goes on living in a way that contradicts what he is as a Christian will become confused and conflicted about who he is (II Peter 1:9)! The same thing will be true of someone who does not *clearly identify with* and *play the role of* his or her gender.

Gender distinction is built into God's creation, and God intends for each gender to fulfill his or her distinct role. God also intends for us to clearly display that distinction through our appearance.

TWO BIBLICAL PRINCIPLES

Anyone who works with young people is concerned about dress issues. Any thinking parent will be proactive about it. Adults should be setting the example for both the youth and for one another on this issue. Most Christians do agree on some level with the principles of modesty (adequately covered) and distinction (not cross-dressing). These are biblical principles that should influence how we dress.

Modesty

As Dr. Rick Flanders has pointed out in his helpful booklet, *Does God Care What I Wear?*, the word *naked* in the Bible almost never means *nude*.[7] Nakedness means *inadequately covered*. Being adequately covered is a principle that reaches back all the way to the Garden of Eden.

> *"And the eyes of them both were opened, and they knew that they were naked; and they sewed fig leaves together, and made themselves aprons."*—Genesis 3:7

> *"Unto Adam also and to his wife did the LORD God make coats of skins, and clothed them."*—Genesis 3:21

Adam and Eve's shame over their unclothed condition was not an issue of immodesty between a husband and wife, but between fallen man and their God (Genesis 3:9-10). God clothed them with "coats" (a full covering), in place of their "aprons" (a partial covering), so that their nakedness would be adequately covered in His presence. The clothing God provided also symbolized the atoning sacrifice for mankind's sin and the righteousness that would be imputed to humanity as a result of it. Man's attempt at atoning for his own sin (aprons of fig leaves) has always been woefully inadequate.

In the Bible, the public removal of clothing, or being inadequately covered in public, is sinful and shameful.

> *"And Noah began to be an husbandman, and he planted a vineyard: And he drank of the wine, and was drunken; and he was uncovered within his tent. And Ham, the father of*

Canaan, saw the nakedness of his father, and told his two brethren without. And Shem and Japheth took a garment, and laid it upon both their shoulders, and went backward, and covered the nakedness of their father; and their faces were backward, and they saw not their father's nakedness."
—Genesis 9:20-23

"…Moses saw that the people were naked; (for Aaron had made them naked unto their shame among their enemies:)"
—Exodus 32:25

"Behold, I am against thee, saith the LORD of hosts; and I will discover thy skirts upon thy face, and I will shew the nations thy nakedness, and the kingdoms thy shame."—Nahum 3:5

"Therefore that disciple whom Jesus loved saith unto Peter, It is the Lord. Now when Simon Peter heard that it was the Lord, he girt his fisher's coat unto him, (for he was naked,) and did cast himself into the sea."—John 21:7

Noah's "uncovered" condition and his son seeing him in that condition were both shameful. The idolatry of the children of Israel led them to public nakedness. Idolatrous practices and the consequences of God's judgment are described throughout the Old Testament prophets as revealing a nation's "nakedness." Peter, a backslidden disciple, was inadequately covered. Before he would stand before the Lord Jesus, he adequately covered himself with "his fisher's coat."

In the church, ladies are to be examples of modest, decent dress accompanied by good works. Her gender is to be specifically highlighted by her attire.

> *"In like manner also, that women adorn themselves in modest apparel, with shamefacedness and sobriety; not with broided hair, or gold, or pearls, or costly array; But (which becometh women professing godliness) with good works."*
> —I Timothy 2:9-10

The word modest means *orderly* or *decorous*. The word shamefacedness means *reverent timidity* or *downcast eyes*, and is used one other time in the New Testament to describe our attitude toward God (Hebrews 12:28). The word sobriety means *soundness of mind* or *sanity*. A woman's attire should be orderly, reflecting a sane understanding of her position in the church. A woman who dresses immodestly (inadequately covered) does not reflect timidity or a sane understanding of herself, especially when in the presence of men.

Adequate covering would at least reflect the Bible standard for covering nakedness (Exodus 28:42, "from the loins [middle-back] even unto the thighs [covering them]") on both men and women; and would include, on women, additional covering above the waist. Articles of clothing that are too tight, though they may cover, would be immodest because of what they still reveal: the physical forms of the natural body.

CHAPTER SIX

Displaying Your Gender, Part 2

"Doth not even nature itself teach you, that, if a man have long hair, it is a shame unto him? But if a woman have long hair, it is a glory to her: for her hair is given her for a covering."
—I Corinthians 11:14-15

"The woman shall not wear that which pertaineth unto a man, neither shall a man put on a woman's garment: for all that do so are abomination unto the LORD thy God."
—Deuteronomy 22:5

Two biblical principles should influence how we dress: *modesty* and *distinction*. Modest attire is the adequate covering of our bodies in response to our fallen condition. Distinct attire is covering that expresses the distinction of our creation.

Distinction

In I Corinthians 11, Paul is starting to address problems with the Corinthian gatherings. He refers to "ordinances" in verse 2. The Greek word is translated "tradition" every other time in the New Testament. The ordinances Paul mentions here include the *traditions* of praying and preaching in the Corinthian church. Many try to assert that the issue at hand is the tradition of women wearing a shawl; but as we will see, the immediate discussion is hair length in the context of appropriate, public worship. Consider six logical reasons why Paul is not referring to a veil, or shawl:

1. A shawl is nowhere mentioned in the passage. If Paul were referring to a shawl, shouldn't he have said so?

2. The Greek words for "covered" (11:6, 7) and "uncovered" (11:5, 13) are not used anywhere else in the New Testament. To make these verbs refer to a shawl has no precedent. Most commentators who take the shawl/veil position refer it to a Jewish custom. There is no reason to assume that a Jewish custom was creating a stir in this predominantly Gentile church.

3. Paul repeatedly uses words that refer to hair and its length (v. 5, "shaven"; v. 6, "shorn" and "shaven"; v. 14, "long hair").

4. If the subject is women wearing shawls, why does Paul point out that the woman's hair is given to her for a covering (v. 15)?

5. The word "covering" in verse 15 probably does mean *veil*. Contrary to what many commentators say, however, the word points *more* to the subject being hair length than a shawl. The Greek phrases translated "having his head covered" (lit. *having down from his head*) and "with her head uncovered" (lit. *not covered down from her head*) obviously relate to length of hair. The point of verse 15, then, is that the hair of a woman has been provided to her (by creation) *in the place of* ("for") a physical covering. The point is *hair*.

6. The opening verse of the discussion clearly refers to hair length. In verse 4, "having his head covered" is literally *having something hanging down from his head*. The point is that hair that hangs down on a man is too long, and hair that does not hang down on a woman is too short.

Hair length, then, is the male and female's natural ability to visibly distinguish their genders. But, even if you believe the issue in I Corinthians 11 was over wearing a shawl, the conclusion is the same: a man or woman who has the appearance of the opposite gender "dishonors his head [authority]." It is dishonoring to God when the visible distinction between male and female is not maintained. Therefore, whenever that visible distinction is disregarded or blurred, the worship is not acceptable.

The conclusion from I Corinthians 11 is only underscored by the prohibition of Deuteronomy 22:5.

> *"The woman shall not wear that which pertaineth unto a man, neither shall a man put on a woman's garment: for all that do so are abomination unto the LORD thy God."*

Many have tried to classify this prohibition into the same category of prohibitions against sowing two different kinds of seeds in the same garden (22:9), plowing with an ox and a donkey together (22:10), or wearing clothing of mixed fibers (22:11). Though all of these prohibitions are found in the same chapter of the Bible (Deuteronomy 22), they are of an entirely different classification.

The key word in this verse is "abomination." God did command Israel to view certain animals *with disgust* (Leviticus 11:10-13, 20, 23, 41-42), even though, as part of His creation, those animals were not an *abomination* to God Himself. But, for a behavior or person to be "an abomination," or an "abomination to the Lord," means that by it, or them, there is some compromise of

God's perfect sacrifice, God's unique position, or God's moral absolutes. Here are a few examples:

> *"Thou shalt not lie with mankind, as with womankind: it is abomination."*—Leviticus 18:22

> *"The graven images of their gods shall ye burn with fire: thou shalt not desire the silver or gold that is on them, nor take it unto thee, lest thou be snared therein: for it is an abomination to the LORD thy God."*—Deuteronomy 7:25

> *"Thou shalt not sacrifice unto the LORD thy God any bullock, or sheep, wherein is blemish, or any evilfavouredness: for that is an abomination unto the LORD thy God."*
> —Deuteronomy 17:1

Some may argue that Old Testament laws were *only* a shadow of the greater reality. They point to some of the laws mentioned previously as merely teaching the general principle of separation (not mixing seeds, not using a donkey and ox together). But even if Deuteronomy 22:5 was a shadow of a greater reality, what would that *greater reality* be? What general principle would it teach? Wouldn't the greater reality have to be the distinction between male and female? At best, wouldn't it refer to the natural differences between male and female?

But it is more than that. The prohibition of Deuteronomy 22:5 is rooted in the natural distinction of Creation. The distinction of genders is an absolute that transcends time, place, and culture. The verse teaches that, in an orderly society, some things pertain to men and some things pertain to women. Any behavior that blurs the natural distinction between men and women compromises God's moral absolute as it relates to gender.

This is a Bible principle that should be considered in every area of our lives (dress, sports, career, positions). We must ask ourselves, "How is what I'm doing (dress, behavior, activity, etc.) actually distinguishing my gender from the other?" We must also not be afraid to ask the question, "*Should* males or females do such-and-such?"

Some would argue that male and female distinction is irrelevant since Christ abolished those distinctions. They quote Galatians 3:28,

> "*There is neither Jew nor Greek, there is neither bond nor free, there is neither male nor female: for ye are all one in Christ Jesus.*"

Those who argue that Galatians 3:28 teaches that Christ has abolished the distinction of male and female get it wrong on two points. First, they are wrong about the interpretation. Galatians 3:28 teaches that there is no difference between male and female *in the matter of salvation*: both have an equal privilege to be saved. Second, they are wrong about salvation. Christ's redemption does not erase God's creative intent; it restores it!

Salvation brings us back into the relationship with God that had been forfeited in the garden. Though we still wrestle with sinful tendencies, we are empowered by the forgiveness of sins and the indwelling Christ to be everything God intended us to be at the beginning!

Clearly displaying our gender is part of being what God intended us to be in the beginning. As male and female, there is an obvious distinction. This distinction is God-ordained. Our roles and our dress should accurately reflect the God-given identity of our creation.

Be what you are; that's what God intended.

At the Heart of the Issue

"I have chosen the way of truth: thy judgments have I laid before me."—Psalm 119:30

"If any man will do his will, he shall know of the doctrine, whether it be of God, or whether I speak of myself."
—John 7:17

Rosaria was a university professor who taught English and women's studies. She was also an outspoken homosexual who aired her complaints against Christianity, Republicans, and what she thought was a male-dominated society. The Bible, she thought, had ruined many good people because they had misinterpreted it. In a 1997 article for a local newspaper, she was going to set the record straight!

As a result of her article, Rosaria received a letter from a pastor confronting her, not with anger, but with challenging questions. *What brought you to these conclusions? Are you sure that you're right about them?* The pastor's searching questions haunted Rosaria. Through this pastor's reaching out to her, Rosaria eventually came to his church where she was confronted with the choice of seeing her homosexuality through the lens of the world, or taking God at His Word, and seeing it through that lens.

> *"I wrestled with the question: Did I really want to understand homosexuality from God's point of view, or did I just want to argue with him?"*

Finally, Rosaria decided to take God at His Word, not only on the issue of homosexuality, but on the issue of salvation as well. When she was ready to trust Jesus as her Lord and Savior, the pastor and his wife were ready to help her with that decision, and their church was ready to welcome a "new creature" into their assembly.[8]

Rosaria's story illustrates two important truths. First, the issue of *what you are* is only rightly addressed by *what God has said*. Feelings and exploration will not help you determine that identity. The crisis she faced was the crux of the entire issue: Will we view gender and everything that comes with it through the lens of the world or through the lens of God's Word? And *Who* has our best interests in mind anyway?

The psalmist's determination was that he would choose the "way of truth" (Psalm 119:30). Have you determined the same? Have you surrendered your life to the truths of God's Word? How will the Bible truths about gender now impact your life in light of that surrender?

The second important truth is that God wants your identity to be *in Christ*. As human beings, we have all broken the laws that God established. The breaking of those laws is called sin. "All have sinned," the Bible tells us, and "the wages of sin is death." Because of our sin, God must punish us. The punishment for breaking the eternal laws of God is eternal suffering in the lake of fire, hell. But Jesus, God the Son, left heaven to be born on the earth. He lived a life we never could and died under God's wrath like we should have. He died in our place. He took our punishment on the cross but rose again three days later! He is alive today, a testimony to His sacrifice on our behalf, and an Advocate for all who will depend upon Him alone for salvation.

When you, as a sinner, cease depending on baptism, being a good person, church membership, or any other religious act, and start depending on Jesus alone, God no longer sees you as you were, but as you are *in Christ*! The simple decision to depend provides us the forgiveness of our sins (they've all been punished on Jesus!) and a home in Heaven. If you've never made that decision, won't you do that right now?

As the world wrestles with questions of gender, God has already provided the answers in His Word and with His Church. God's purpose is that on *all* issues, the lost would find their answers in a testifying people. Israel was to be that people in the Old Testament; the Church is that people today. Let us not, as the Church, fail to show and tell God's answers to the world's questions on this important issue of gender.

NOTES

[1] "Are these the most PC parents in the world? The couple raising a 'genderless baby'... to protect his (or her) right to choice," <u>Mail Online</u>, 24 May, 2011, 8 Mar. 2013 <http://www.dailymail.co.uk/news/article-1389593/Kathy-Witterick-David-Stocker-raising-genderless-baby.html>

[2] "Gender and Gender Identity," <u>Planned Parenthood</u>, 1 Mar. 2013 <http://www.plannedparenthood.org/health-topics/sexual-orientation-gender/gender-gender-identity-26530.htm>

[3] David Crary, "Gallup Study: 3.4 Percent of US Adults are LGBT," <u>WTOP</u>, 18 Oct. 2012, 19 Oct. 2012 <http://www.wtop.com//209/3083798/Gallup-study-34-percent-of-US-adults-are-LGBT>

[4] Sam Dillon, "Harvard Chief Defends His Talk on Women," <u>New York Times</u>, 18 Jan. 2005, 13 Mar. 2013 <http://www.nytimes.com/2005/01/18/national/18harvard.html>

[5] Consider these reports: Salynn Boyles, "What Makes Wives Happy?" WebMD, 1 Mar. 2006, 18 Mar. 2013 < http://www.webmd.com/balance/news/20060301/what-makes-wives-happy>; Lisa Miller, "The Retro Wife," <u>New York Magazine</u>, 17 Mar. 2013, 21 Mar. 2013 <http://www.nymag.com/news/features/retro-wife-2013-3>

[6] Michael Dobbs, "Harvard Chief's Comments on Women Assailed," <u>The Washington Post</u>, 19 Jan. 2005, 13 Mar. 2013 <http://www.washingtonpost.com/wp-dyn/articles/A19181-2005Jan18.html>

[7] Rick Flanders, <u>Does God Care About What I Wear?</u> (Murfreesboro: Bill Rice Ranch, Inc., 2012) 13.

[8] Rosaria Champagne Butterfield, "My Train Wreck Conversion," <u>Christianity Today</u>, 7 Feb. 2013, 22 Feb. 2013 <http://www.christianitytoday.com/ct/2013/january-february/my-train-wreck-conversion.html>